T0135733

Logic and Computations

Compact companion

Herman Ruge Jervell
University of Oslo

Bibliographic information published by the Deutsche Nationalbibliothek

The Deutsche Nationalbibliothek lists this publication in the Deutsche
Nationalbibliografie; detailed bibliographic data are available
in the Internet at http://dnb.d-nb.de.

ISBN 978-3-8325-3090-7

Logos Verlag Berlin GmbH
Comeniushof, Gubener Str. 47,
10243 Berlin
Tel.: +49 (0)30 42 85 10 90
Fax: +49 (0)30 42 85 10 92
INTERNET: http://www.logos-verlag.de

Contents

Preface

These are notes from the course in logic and computation in computer science at the University of Oslo. The students are assumed to have a first course in discrete mathematics — but not much more. The notations used here are standard and the results in this book are standard. The originality is more in the development of the material. You will meet

- Automata theory

- Describing computations in logic

- Using turing machines

- Predicate logic with completeness and incompleteness

- Complexity

This is usually treated in much longer textbooks. We emphasize the use of logic to describe computations. This is particularly useful when it comes to where the theory is applied in computer science. But it also gives an introduction to the incompleteness phenomena. Another theme is to introduce computations using disjunctive and conjunctive non-determinism. This appears in various places

- As alternating automata

- As introduction to sequential calculus

- As introduction to the complexity classes NP and PSPACE

A university course has often two agendas — an open and a hidden. The open agenda gives the theories, tools and the applications to be learned. But in addition to the open agenda there is also a hidden agenda. The students have to learn how to argue about and how to remember the open agenda. One of the difficulties are to teach the students how large the steps in the arguments have to be and to learn a memorable core of the theory. The compact companion should remind the students of the hidden agenda — it gives a memorable core for the students learning logic and computation. But the companion should be supplemented with exercises, more material, lectures so that the students could climb up to the mastery of the material presented here.

Here is a list of some of the pioneers: Gottlob Frege, Axel Thue, Thoralf Skolem, Kurt Gödel, Emil Post, Gerhard Gentzen, Alan Turing, Stephen Kleene. They have contributed to the themes covered here in a number of ways. You should look at the web to be informed about their contributions. Since these lectures were given in Oslo I would like to emphasize the contributions of Axel Thue and Thoralf Skolem as professors at the University of Oslo. Thue introduced formal grammars and the use of trees in their treatment. He also introduced the Thue word. Skolem made contributions to all parts of logic. They were both lonely pioneers — they hardly lectured on these subjects and had few students — many of their contributions were rediscovered by others.

Manuscript is produced with LaTeX, and the packages memoir and tikz.

Introduction

The theme

We study computations and learn how to describe them, and argue about them. The simplest picture of a computation is as follows

IN  OUT

All our computations and machines are discrete. Input is a word in a finite alphabet. Output could be a word or it could be a Boolean value — yes / no. We shall investigate sequential computations. The computations are performed in discrete steps thought about as follows

- the machine is in a configuration

- it may read a symbol from the input word

- then the machine goes over into a new configuration

The transition is done by following some simple rule — often given in a program for the machine. The computation continues — step for step — until it terminates.

Now there are two quite different perspectives on machines

Intensional We can look at the machines as given by its program — the rules for how to go from one configuration to the next

Extensional We can look at the machine as a function which transforms an input to an output

One of the themes in this book is the gap between the two perspectives. There is no easy way from an extensional specification of a machine to an intensional program realising it — or the other way. Often it is useful to think of oneself as a machine doing the computation. We imagine ourselves as small persons inside the machines doing the computations — and become aware of how restrictions on memory and time affects the computations.

Another perspective is to look at the machines as syntax machines. They have as input a word and then have transition rules which tell us how to get from a configuration to the next. Each configuration can be written as a word and the transition rules give syntactical transformations. This perspective leads us to the formal grammars.

And yet another perspective is to look at the description of the computation. We can describe the result of a computation as

$$\textbf{START} \wedge \textbf{TRANSITIONS} \rightarrow \textbf{FINAL}$$

And the existence of a computation by

$$\textbf{START} \wedge \textbf{TRANSITIONS} \wedge \textbf{FINAL}$$

Then we are interested in

- A logical language sufficient to describe computations

- A logical calculus such that the first sentence above can be derived if and only if we have a computation going from START to FINAL, and the second sentence satisfied if and only if there exists a computation going from START to FINAL.

We shall start with some examples of machines with a finite number of states and look at the computations they are able to do. The development will be in the chapters after this introduction, but we recommend to look at the examples and see how they can be captured in a more formal way.

Switch

We are in a room with a push button switch and a lamp and have the following machine

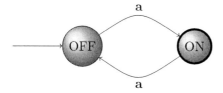

- the input alphabet is {a} — corresponding to a push on the button

- there are two states — **OFF** and **ON**

- the start state is **OFF** — marked with an arrow into **OFF**

- from each state we have an arrow labeled **a** to the other state

- the state **ON** is marked with a double ring — it is called a final state

- as input we have words in the alphabet — a sequence of pushes on the button

This is a simple example of a DFA — a deterministic finite state automaton.

Parity

We make an automaton which can decide whether there are an odd or even 1's in a binary number.

- the input alphabet is $\{0, 1\}$

- there are two states — **O** and **E**

- the start state is **E** — it is also the final state

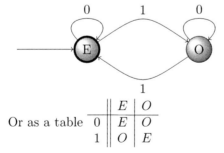

Or as a table

		E	O
0		E	O
1		O	E

Producer and consumer

We have two actions — to produce and to consume a chocolate.
The machine may store up to three chocolates. We have input
alphabet $\{p, c\}$ and the following DFA

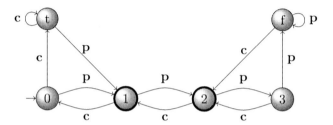

Here we have decided on the actions of the machine when we
try to consume when there are 0 chocolates and when we try to
produce when we have 3 chocolates — and also on which states
are final.

Searching in words

We look at words in the alphabet $\{a, b\}$ and try to find out
whether they contain the subword *abba*. We do this by nondeterministically waiting until *abba* comes. The following nondeterministic automaton does the job

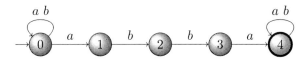

On some of the arrows we have two labels — this is just a shorthand for two arrows with one label at each. The essential work is done within state 0. There we wait and wait. Whenever we meet an a we can nondeterministically jump to 1 — or continue our waiting in state 0. A word is accepted if there is a run which ends in the final state 4.

This is interesting. There is a simple procedure from a given word w to construct a nondeterministic automaton accepting words containing w as a subword. Later we shall show that this non-deterministic automaton can be replaced by a deterministic one.

The chocolate game

Above we had *disjunctive* nondeterminism — there is a choice of arrows out and we had to find one which leads to success. We can also have a *conjunctive* nondeterminism — there is a choice of arrows out and we must show that all choices lead to success. We model this with graphs with two types of nodes — disjunctive which are round and conjunctive nodes which are square.

Consider now a game where we start with 5 chocolates and 2 players — Alice and Bob. Either player can take either 1 or 2 chocolates. They alternate with Alice starting. The one who takes the last chocolate wins. Here is the game from Alices point of view. There is only one kind of transition — to take either 1 or 2 chocolates — and we have not bothered to write down the label on the arrows.

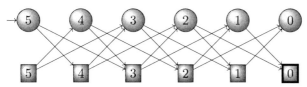

Alice sees that if she takes 2 chocolates she has a strategy for winning.

This leads to the notion of AFA — alternating finite state automata.

Grammar of parentheses

The following is a grammar for well formed parentheses

Startsymbol: S
Terminal alphabet: ( )
Non terminal alphabet : S

$$S \rightarrow SS$$
$$S \rightarrow (S)$$
$$S \rightarrow ()$$

A derivation within the grammar

$$\frac{S}{\frac{SS}{\frac{(S)S}{\frac{(())S}{(())()}}}}$$

This derivation shows that $(())()$ is a wellformed expression within the grammar. We start with the symbol S and then at each step we apply one of the rules — replacing a left hand side with a righthand side.

Thue word

In the grammar above we did the computation in a sequential way — we only applied the rule at one instance at the time. We have another system where we apply the rules simultaneously to a number of places. Here is the derivation of the famous Thue word where we at each step applies the rules as much as possible.

Startsymbol: a
Alphabet: a b

$$a \rightarrow ab$$
$$b \rightarrow ba$$

And the derivation

$$\frac{a}{\begin{array}{c}\underline{ab}\\\underline{abba}\\\underline{abbabaab}\\abbabaabbaababba\end{array}}$$

Here the computation goes on and on. This gives an arbitrary long word

$$abbabaabbaababba\ldots$$

Let us write for the partial Thue words and the infinite Thue word

$$\tau_0 = a$$
$$\tau_1 = ab$$
$$\tau_2 = abba$$
$$\tau_3 = abbabaab$$
$$\ldots$$
$$\ldots$$
$$\tau = abbabaabbaababba\ldots$$

We can use the parity automaton above to give an alternative development of the Thue word. The following procedure gives the n'th symbol

- Write n as binary number

- If it has an even number of 1's, write a, else write b

The Thue word does not repeat itself — one can prove there are no subword of the form uuu. The proof of this is rather heavy and we have put a sketch of it in a box — for the eager to read.

It is sufficient to prove that there are no subword of the form $cwcwc$ where c is a single symbol — either a or b

1. At positions $2n + 1$ and $2n + 2$ we have either ab or ba

2. All subwords starting from an odd position and ending in an even position have equally many a's as b's

3. There are no subwords of form aaa or bbb

4. We get from τ_{n+1} to τ_n by erasing all symbols at even positions

5. We get from τ_{n+1} to τ_n by erasing all symbols at odd positions and then interchange a and b

6. Assume we have a subword $cwcwc$ with c either a and b and of minimal length

7. If w is of even length, then the first c must be at an even or an odd position. In both cases the subwords cwc and w must contain equally many a's and b's. This is impossible.

8. If w is of odd length, then the c's must be all at either even or odd positions. By erasing the symbols at the other positions (and leaving the c's) we get a subword $cvcvc$ which is of shorter length contradicting the minimal length assumption for $cwcwc$.

Life

Imagine that we have an infinite number of cells in a plane

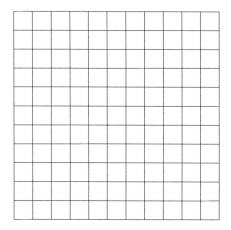

Here we have drawn a finite part of it. Each cell can be either **dead** or **alive**. We have colored the cells which are alive. We could have the following configuration

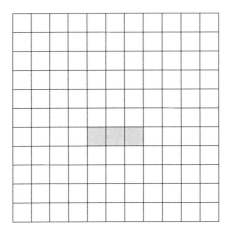

Each cell has 8 neighbors. The configuration is changed from one generation to the next by the following rule

> **Survival:** Either 2 or 3 alive neighbors
>
> **Birth:** 3 alive neighbors

This means that the next generation of the configuration above will be

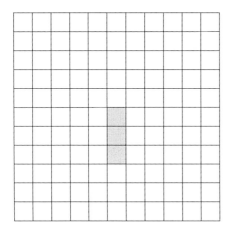

And the generation after it will return to the previous generation. One can make complicated computations with Life. In fact it is possible to use Life to simulate any computation on a turing machine. This is described in the remarkable books "Winning ways" by Berlekamp, Conway and Guy.

The Thue word and Life are examples of non-sequential computations. In this book we shall concentrate on sequential computations. In the computations there are active parts which are changed from one generation to the next and passive parts which are not changed. In the Thue word and in Life the active parts are spread throughout the compuational medium. In the sequential computations the active parts are local.

Automata 1

We start with the simplest type of machines. They are discrete and sequential — and their only memory is hard wired. Remember the basic situation

IN ———————→ MACHINE ———————→ OUT

As input we have words in a finite alphabet. The machine reads the word — one symbol at each step — and then do something. It is useful to make this situation more human. There is a small man inside the machine

IN ———————→ [☖] ———————→ OUT

This small man — called the turing man — receives symbols from the word and does something. To construct such a machine we need the following ingredients

Input: This is a word in a finite alphabet — so a finite sequence of symbols

Output: For simplicity we usually restricts ourselves to YES/NO

Configuration: What the turing man must know at each step to perform the computation

In finite state machine there is only a finite set of configurations. If we suddenly stop the computation, then the configuration contains all the information that the turing man need to know to continue the computation at some later time. If we have a mechanical machine consisting of many parts, then the turing man must know how each part is. So the number of configurations may be quite large. The one thing which is not involved is the history of configurations. The turing man need not know how the configurations have developed over time, but only how they are at the moment.

This gives the simplest type of computation. A switch is an example. In a large computing system there will often be many parts that can be described as automata.

1.1 DFA

A deterministic finite state automaton (DFA) is given by

Alphabet: A finite input alphabet $\mathcal{A}$

States: A finite set of states $\mathcal{Q}$

Transitions: A function $\delta : \mathcal{A} \times \mathcal{Q} \to \mathcal{Q}$

Start state: An element $q \in \mathcal{Q}$ — also called an initial state

Final states: A subset $\mathcal{T} \subseteq \mathcal{Q}$ — also called accepting states or terminal states

In a DFA the configurations are the states. The DFA is

Deterministic: The transitions are uniquely given by the symbol read and the state — and it gives the next state.

Finite state: We have a finite number of states. They are given when we define the automaton.

We have two different ways of presenting a DFA

- as labeled directed graph — examples of this are the switch and the producer/consumer given in the introduction

- as a function table for the transitions in addition to alphabet, states, initial state and terminal states

In the introduction we considered the switch automaton

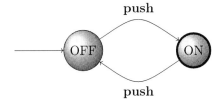

This can also be given as

Alphabet: { push }

States: { on , off }

Transitions:

	on	off
push	off	on

Start: off

Final: { on }

One way to think of the computation on a DFA is that the input word forces the turing machine to wander through states. Each input word gives a path through the states.

Exercise 1.1 *Given a DFA with N states and an input word w of length $> N$. Then some state must be visited more than once.*

Another way to look at automata is to look at them as coloring devices. Consider the states as different colors. Take for example the colors of the switching automaton to be black for **on** and gray for **off**. Then the word consisting of six pushes is colored as follows

push   **push**   push   **push**   push   **push**

We start with the first push to be colored gray and then use the transitions to get the whole word colored.

1.2 NFA

The DFA's have discovered by many people. The NFA — non deterministic finite automata — was defined by Dana Scott and Michael Rabin in 1958.

In non determinism the states are choice points. There are two quite different choices which can be made

Disjunctive: We must find an acceptable choice

Conjunctive: We must check that all choices are acceptable

In an NFA we have the first type of choice points. Given an input word w, there are many possible runs through the states. Each choice point gives a branching and a word is accepted if there is an accepted run. Formally we can define an NFA by changing the definition of DFA slightly to: In a DFA there is to each symbol and each state a unique transition — a unique arrow to a next state. In an NFA we change the transition part of the definition of DFA to

Transitions: $\rho : (\mathcal{A} \cup \{\varepsilon\}) \times \mathcal{Q} \times \mathcal{Q} \to \textbf{BOOLE}$

This is a generalization of DFA:

- there may be more than 1 or perhaps no arrows labeled with the symbol

- we may have arrows labeled with ε. They give transitions where we do not consume a symbol to follow the arrow.

Non determinism can be used to simulate that we do not know, or that the turing man just chooses something himself.

The NFA used in searching for *abba* has a very useful non determinism. The turing man guesses where the subword begins and then follows the transitions deterministically after having made the guess. We say that a word is accepted in an NFA if there is some run which is accepted. We have a disjunctive non determinism.

In an NFA we can think of a transition as a function from a symbol and a state to a set of states. After having started the computation of a word in an NFA, we can see at each step all the states which can be reached. This gives the idea for how to transform an NFA into a DFA.

Given an NFA with the following

- alphabet $\mathcal{A}$

- states $\mathcal{Q}$

- NFA-transition $\delta : \mathcal{A} \times \mathcal{Q} \to \wp\mathcal{Q}$

- initial state $s \in \mathcal{Q}$

- final states $\mathcal{T} \subseteq \mathcal{Q}$

We introduce a macrostate as a subset of the states $\mathcal{Q}$. The new DFA will walk through macrostates. We define it with

- alphabet $\mathcal{A}$

- macrostates $\wp\mathcal{Q}$

- transition $\Delta : \mathcal{A} \times \wp\mathcal{Q} \to \wp\mathcal{Q}$ given by $\Delta(a, \mathcal{R}) = \bigcup\{\delta(a, r) | r \in \mathcal{R}\}$

- initial state — the macro state $\{s\}$

- final states — all macrostates which intersects $\mathcal{T}$

This defines a DFA doing the same as the NFA. It is a natural construction. Remember the configurations — what we must remember if we suddenly stops the computation. In an NFA we must remember in each instance the set of states we might have come to — that is the macrostates above.

Exercise 1.2 *Convert the NFA that search for abba to a DFA.*

Exercise 1.3 *Show that an NFA with N states can always be converted to a DFA with 2^N states. We may risk an exponential blow up.*

Exercise 1.4 *Often we do not require in a DFA that we have exactly one arrow out in each node for each symbol. Say that we only require that there is at most only one arrow out. Then we formally have an NFA. But if we now do the subset construction we get a DFA with only one extra state. What does this extra state correspond to?*

The disjunctive non determinism is useful to model computations where we must make guesses along the way. We have seen an example with the computation involved in searching for a word.

1.3   AFA

We have introduced both conjunctive and disjunctive choices. The finite state machine using this is called an AFA — alternating finite state automaton. We change the nodes and the acceptance part of the NFA

Nodes: The nodes are partitioned into two parts — the conjunctive nodes (written as squares) and the disjunctive nodes (written as circles)

Acceptance: From the nodes there may be more than one arrow with a given label leading out. For acceptance we require for the conjunctive nodes that all the appropriate arrows leads to acceptance, for the disjunctive nodes that one of the appropriate nodes leads to acceptance.

The chocolate game from the introduction is an AFA

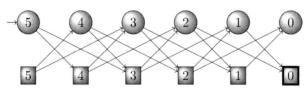

This is a typical use of an AFA. We have two players — Alice who tries to win and Bob who tries to make Alice not win. So Alice must make the good guesses so that she wins no matter which choices Bob makes.

The chocolate game can be considered as a finite state automaton. In the diagram we have written out the transitions. We must also specify

- The alphabet { **take** }

- States: The 12 states from the diagram

- Transitions: The arrows from the diagram

- Start: The round state 5

- Final: The square state 0

The word **take take take** is accepted. We leave you to find a strategy for Alice.

Exercise 1.5 *Consider the chocolate game automaton* $\mathcal{G}$

1. *Write down an AFA which does the opposite of* $\mathcal{G}$

2. *Where is the nondeterminism and what happens there during the runs*

3. *Use macrostates to get rid of the conjunctive non-determinism and get an NFA — and from the NFA use macrostates again to get down to a DFA*

4. *How many states are in the DFA*

Problem 1.6 *Explain how we can use AFA to simulate 2-person games. What corresponds to the two players and what is a winning strategy for the first and for the second player.*

1.4   Subsets of words

In our computations we looked at situations

IN ────────────────→ MACHINE ────────────────→ YES/NO

or

WORDS ────────────────────────────→ YES/NO

or as classification of the universe of words

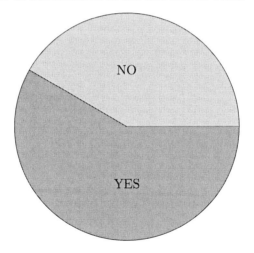

The finite state machines carve out subsets in the universe of words — some words are accepted and others are not. And with simple operations on the machines we can perform boolean operations on these subsets of words.

Complement

This is simple for a DFA — just interchange the accepted and the non accepted states. A word which was previously accepted becomes not accepted — and conversely. And that is exactly what we need to take complement.

Exercise 1.7 *Discuss why it is more difficult to take complements for NFA's and simple for AFA's.*

Union and intersection

Assume we have two automata $\mathcal{A}$ and $\mathcal{B}$ which carves out subsets of words in the same alphabet. We can use a disjunctive node to first guess which automaton to use and get the union machine

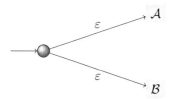

and with a conjunctive node the intersection machine

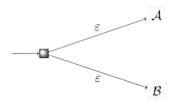

Exercise 1.8 *Assume we have two DFA's — A with a states and B with b states and that they both use the same alphabet. Estimate the number of states for a union and an intersection machine*

1.5   REG

We now look further into the subsets of words. The regular expressions was introduced by Stephen Kleene as a way to explain what was going on with the words fed into the automata. In logic he is more known for his many contributions to computation theory, but the regular expressions with the use of Kleene star is the more widely known.

Given an alphabet Σ. The regular expressions $\mathcal{R}$ over Σ are given by

$$\mathcal{R} :: a \mid \varepsilon \mid \emptyset \mid (\mathcal{R} \vee \mathcal{R}) \mid (\mathcal{R} \circ \mathcal{R}) \mid (\mathcal{R}^\star) \text{ where } a \text{ from } \Sigma$$

We call them

disjunction: $\lor$

concatenation: $\circ$

star: $\star$

The regular expressions give sets of words from the alphabet Σ as follows

- $\overline{a} = \{a\}$
- $\overline{\varepsilon} = \{\varepsilon\}$
- $\overline{\emptyset} = \{\ \}$
- $\overline{R \lor S} = \overline{R} \cup \overline{S}$
- $\overline{R \circ S} = \{\rho\sigma | \rho \in \overline{R}, \sigma \in \overline{S}\}$
- $\overline{R^\star} = \{\varepsilon\} \cup \overline{R} \cup \overline{R \circ R} \cup \overline{R \circ R \circ R} \cup \cdots$

Note the difference between ε and $\emptyset$. Often we omit the concatenation symbol $\circ$. We let the operation be bound in order — star, concatenation and union — and will often omit superfluous parentheses.

Remember the picture of a computation

IN $\longrightarrow$ MACHINE $\longrightarrow$ OUT

and our two perspectives

Intensional We can look at the machines as given by its program — the rules for how to go from one configuration to the next

Extensional We can look at the machine as a function which transforms an input to an output

So far we have mostly looked at the automata from the intensional point of view. We have seen how to describe them giving rules for how we get from one configuration to the next. This is what one could call the operational semantics of the automata. In the extensional perspective we are more interested in the set of inputwords which are accepted. We can use regular expressions to describe them and get a denotational semantics. It turns out that finite state automata and regular expressions describe the same computations. The regular expressions give exactly the subsets of words which the finite state automata are able to carve out.

Exercise 1.9 *Consider words in the alphabet $\{a, b\}$. Give regular expressions for the following sets of words in the alphabet:*

1. *Words ending in aa*

2. *Words not ending in aa*

3. *Words containing an even number of a's*

4. *Words ending in abba*

5. *Words containing the subword abba*

6. Words not containing the subword abba

We show that we can go from REG to NFA and back. As a help we generalize the NFA to allow regular expressions as labels on the arrows.

From REG to NFA

We start with a regular expression σ in our alphabet. This corresponds to the following generalized NFA:

Then we break down the regular expressions on the labels by replacing transitions with nodes over simpler transitions as follows:

Concatenation:

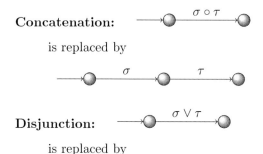

is replaced by

Disjunction:

is replaced by

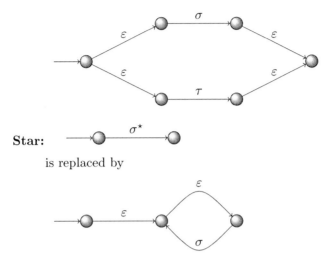

Star:

is replaced by

In this way we get after a while an ordinary NFA.

From NFA to REG

Given an NFA. We start with adding a startstate and a single final state using ε-transitions. So the NFA looks like

where all the machinery is inside the rectangle. Then we eliminate the nodes inside the rectangle at the expense of using regular expressions as transitions. The crucial case is the following. Say we have the following three states with transitions

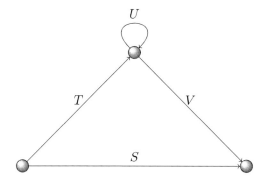

we can replace this with

$$S \vee TU^\star V$$

To get rid of a single node we must do this simultaneously for all triangles going through this node. In this way we get rid of all the nodes in the rectangle and get a single transition from start to finish labeled with a large regular expression. This is the regular expression corresponding to the NFA we started with.

1.6   Minimal DFA

If we now look at the basic situation

IN ————————→ MACHINE ————————→ OUT

we feed the machine with words from an alphabet. The words forces some changes in the internal configurations of the machine — for a finite state machine it forces a walk through states. To what extent can we find about the inner workings of the machine from the effect that the input words have on the machine?

Definition 1.1 *A state in a DFA is accessible, if there is some word which gives a path from the start state to it. Two states are distinguishable if there is a word which forces one state to be accepted and the other to not be accepted. Two states are n-distinguishable if there is a word of length $\leq n$ which makes them distinguishable.*

There is a simple way to classify which states are not distinguishable

- write down a table of all pair of states

- write down a 0 for all pairs which are 0-distinguishable — those are the pairs of states where one is accepted and the other is not

- assume we have found all the pairs which are 0, 1, ..., n-distinguishable and we have written 0, 1, ..., n in the table. A pair is $n+1$-distinguishable if there is a transition which makes them n-distinguishable.

- after a while this process terminates — we do not get any new distinguishable pairs. The table give then the indistinguishable pairs

And we have a simple way for a given DFA to find a minimal DFA doing the same

- delete all nodes which are not accessible

- let the new nodes be the equivalence classes of the indistinguishable pairs

1.7 Pumping lemma

A DFA $\mathcal{A}$ has just a finite number of states. Say it has N states. A word fed into $\mathcal{A}$ will force a path through the states and if the word is longer than N, some state must be visited more than once. This is the crucial observation behind the pumping lemma.

Lemma 1.2 (Pumping) *Given a DFA $\mathcal{A}$ with N states and a word w of length $> N$ which is accepted. Then we can partition w into $w = xyz$ where the length of y is non empty, and such that all words from $x(y)^\star z$ are also accepted.*

Proof. The word w gives rise to a path through the states of the automaton

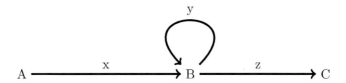

We go through the states starting with A, then go to B and take a loop to get to B again as the first state which we meets twice. After having visited B the second time we continue to C. The state B gives the partition $w = xyz$. But then we also get from A to C using words:

$$xz \ , \ xyz \ , \ xyyz \ , \ xyyyz \ \cdots$$

All words $x(y)^\star z$ go from A to C. If one of them is accepted, then all of them are. ∎

Exercise 1.10 *Show that there are no DFA which can check whether expressions in ( ) are correct parenthesis expressions.*

Exercise 1.11 *Consider the Thue words*

$$ab \ , \ abba \ , \ abbabaab \ \cdots$$

Show that there is no DFA which can check whether a word in a b is a Thue word or not.

Problem 1.12 *Discuss why the pumping lemma says that a DFA with N states can only count up to N.*

1.8   PDA

With our finite state machines we have characterized computations where we can give an account in advance of what can be
remembered. The pushdown automata go beyond that. There
we can both remember the state and also part of the history. Let
us see some details of the buildup. We start with an inputtape
and a controller reading it, add a stack and get

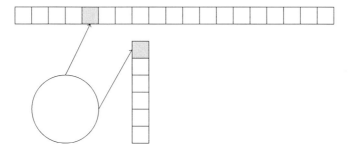

Input tape: The horizontal tape on top. It can only be read
from left to right.

Stack: The vertical tape on the right. It has a read / write head
to the top of the tape. It can read the topmost symbol,
sense whether the stack is empty, pop off a symbol from a
non-empty stack, write new symbol on top. The operation
is often called top, empty, pop and push.

Controller: A finite state machine which acts on the input
tape and the stack.

I have colored the two active squares. On the tape we read a symbol and then move to the square to the right. On the stack we read the topmost square and then take away the square and then put a word on the top.

With no stack we get a finite state automaton. The stack makes it different and it is important that we are allowed to let the stack grow arbitrarily high. How high depends on the input and there are no reason to restrict the height in advance. To define a PDA (push down automaton) we must fix

Input alphabet: A finite alphabet $\mathcal{I}$

Stack alphabet: A finite alphabet $\mathcal{S}$

States: A finite set of states $\mathcal{Q}$

Start: A starting state. At the start the stack is empty.

Transitions: More about this below. We only consider nondeterministic computations.

Acceptance: A set of accepting states $\mathcal{A} \subseteq \mathcal{Q}$. A word is accepted if there is a run which ends in an accepting state with an empty stack.

Now to the transitions. Each transition can be written as an arrow between states. We divide up the description into two parts separated by semicolon

Guard: The guard is an element of $(\mathcal{I} \cup \{\varepsilon\}) \times (\mathcal{S} \cup \{\varepsilon\})$. These are the condition which must be satisfied to use the arrow.

Whether the guard condition is satisfied is found out by looking at the two active squares. We must indicate the inputsymbol and the stacksymbol to be read or possibly ε indicating no symbol.

Action: A word from the stack alphabet $\mathcal{S}^\star$ which are put on the top of the stack.

Our PDA is nondeterministic. We may have ε-transitions and there may be more than one arrow out from a state with the same guard.

A useful PDA is the one which checks parentheses.

$), (; \varepsilon$ $(, \varepsilon; ($

This PDA has parenthesis ( ) as symbols in the input alphabet and the stack alphabet — the stack alphabet only needs (. There is only one state which is both the start state and an accepting state. Then it does the following

- If it reads (, it pushes it on top of the stack.

- If it reads) and there is (on top of the stack, it pops it from the stack.

We have acceptance if we ends up with an empty stack. As long as we have space enough for a large stack, then this computation is very fast.

One state is enough for PDA's

In a PDA we have memory in two places — as states and in the stack. The stack may be arbitrary high, but the number of states is bounded. Say we have a PDA $\mathcal{P}$ with Q states. We get a new PDA with only one state by

- keeping the input alphabet

- extending the stack alphabet so that the topsymbol indicates both the state and the top of the stack

1.9   Formal grammars

A formal grammar consists of

- A terminal alphabet $\mathcal{T}$ — often written with small letters

- A nonterminal alphabet $\mathcal{N}$ — often written with capital letters

- A startsymbol $S \in \mathcal{N}$

- A finite set of rules $\mathcal{R}$. Each rule is of the form $\sigma \to \tau$ where σ and τ are words built up from the terminals and the non-terminals and σ contains at least one non-terminal

An application of the rule $\sigma \to \tau$ to the word W consists of replacing one σ in W with τ. A word in the terminal alphabet cannot be further transformed — we need a word with a non-terminal to apply one of the rules.

We have previously seen the grammar for the parenthesis language

Startsymbol: S
Terminal alphabet: ( )
Non terminal alphabet : S

$$S \to SS$$
$$S \to (S)$$
$$S \to ()$$

Here it is important that we have a single non-terminal on the left hand side. We get two important special cases of formal grammars

Context free grammar (CFG): The left hand side of the rules consists of a single non-terminal

Regular grammar (REG): Context free grammar where on the right hand side there is at most one non-terminal and it occurs at the end

The parenthesis language is given by a CFG. It is not regular. The first rule has two non-terminals on the left hand side, and the second rule does have a non-terminal inside the word.

The derivations in a CFG can naturally be written in tree form. Here is a derivation of $(())()$

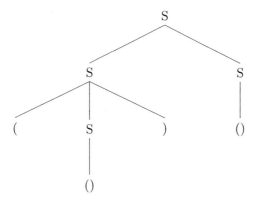

The non-terminals are on the interior nodes of the tree and the leaf nodes contain the terminals. The derived word can be read off on the leaf nodes from left to right. This tree representation gives some interesting opportunities

- Given a word w of terminals. Then we would like to know whether w can be derived. So we must construct a derivation tree with w on the leaf nodes. The grammarians say that we find a parse.

- Does a word w has a unique derivation? Is there only one derivation tree with w at the leaf nodes. The grammarians say that we have a unique parse, there is no ambiguity.

- Given a derivation of a word w. If the word is long, then there must be a long path from the root down to the leaves. This long path contains non-terminals at the nodes and some non-terminal must appear more than once if the path is long enough. This gives rise to a pumping lemma for CFG and can be used to show that languages like $a^n b^n c^n$ are not CFG.

Problem 1.13 (Pumping) *The proof of the pumping lemma for DFA uses that if the input word w is longer than the number of states, then some states must be repeated. There must be a loop and we can use the loop to get many other words which behaves like w. In a CFG we compare the length $|w|$ of the input word with the number of non terminals n and the branching b in the tree. If $|w| > b^n$, then we can find a branch in the derivation of w where some non terminal is repeated. We have the following situation*

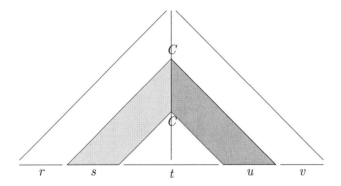

*We have streched out the word w at the bottom of the deriva-
tion tree. There must be a branch where a non terminal C re-
peats itself. This gives a partition w = rstuv where we can
assume that not both s and u are empty. But we have then also
valid representation where we can repeat the colored parts 0, 1,
2 or more times. So we get*

- $w = rstuv$

- $|su| > 0$

- $rs^n tu^n v$ *are also accepted for each n*

*Below is the situation where we have pumped up s and u
twice:*

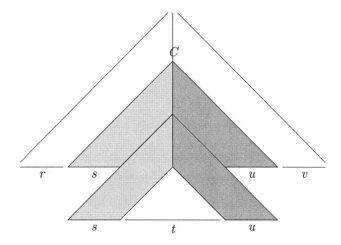

You can use this to show that the language $a^n b^n c^n$ cannot be described by a CFG, nor can the language of Thue words. Discuss why the CFG languages can be seen as languages with a parenthesis structure.

Problem 1.14 *Every CFG can be found with a non deterministic PDA. This is a common problem in parsing. We try to find whether a word can be derived in a CFG by trying to construct a derivation tree of it. This construction can be done by a non deterministic PDA.*

Problem 1.15 *Every PDA gives rise to a CFG. We first construct a PDA with only one state. Then we get a grammar — each arrow gives a rule.*

1.10 More automata

There are a number of automata which we could have looked closer at — but we have chosen not to do it.

Transducers

Transducers are finite state machine where the output is a word — not just a boolean value. In many situations this is the useful concept. The input forces the turing man to wander through the states following the arrows — and we can produce the output symbols either by connecting them to the states (Moore machine) or to the arrows (Mealy machine).

Tree automata

Instead of finite words as input, we have finite trees.

Stream automata

Instead of having a finite word as input we could have an infinite stream. This works fine except that we must adjust for what to take as acceptance. The stream forces in a run the turing man to wander through the states in a DFA. In a computer system we are for example interested in the stream coming from a keyboard. A device gives an input stream. We are rarely interested in the case where we ends up in a single state. Of more interest is the case where we can always reach a certain state — no matter how the input stream has been so far. We could also be interested in the case where an infinite stream visits a certain state infinitely many times, or the set of states which are visited infinitely often.

Neural nets

We can regard a neural net or an electronic circuit as an automaton. They are built up from neurons which looks like

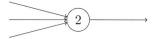

Here we have three input wires and one output wire and the threshold 2. In each wire in each instant there either is or is

not a pulse. The neuron will fire a pulse in the output wire whenever it has received at least 2 pulses the instant before. From such neurons we can build large circuits which are DFA's and conversely it can be shown that the circuits can be used to simulate an arbitrary DFA.

Cellular automata

Life and the Thue word are examples where we have activities which happens all around a board (Life) or a word (Thue word). Here we have parallel automata which go beyond the DFA's and the PDA's.

Markov processes

Here we assign probabilities to the transitions in an NFA — and from an input word we get a distribution of probabilities for reaching the different states.

Descriptions

2.1 Logic as a description language

Let us remind us of how to use logic as a language.

Signature: This gives the names of the relation symbols and the function symbols with their arity (number of arguments). Arity 0 gives constant symbols.

Structure: We use structures for interpretation of sentences — they give a universe and interpretation of the symbols in the signature.

Requirement of the structure: The minimal requirement is that the universe is a non empty set. Below we shall look at extra requirements that the structure gives a finite chain. More about this below.

The signature and the structure gives the parts of the language that we need to interpret for sentences to be true or false. This could be called the non logical part of the language. We have also a logical part — consisting of symbols which have a fixed interpretation

Connectives: $\bot \top \neg \wedge \vee \rightarrow \leftarrow \leftrightarrow$

Quantifiers: $\forall \exists$ — usually the quantifiers are first order and are over elements in the universe. We may also have second order quantifiers — which may range over relations or functions.

We also have parentheses and variables. A formula may contain free variables, in sentences all variables are bound. Given an interpretation a sentence have a truth value. Using the separation between the logical and the non logical symbols we define for a sentence

Valid: True in all interpretations

Satisfiable: There is an interpretation where it is true

Falsifiable: There is an interpretation where it is false

Contradictory: False in all interpretations

One of the lessons learned in logic is the importance of the language — both to be precise about the signature and finding the signature as the first step in making an application.

We now want to use logic to describe computations. A computation is given by the following ingredients

Start: The starting configuration

Transitions: The rules for passing from one configuration to the next

Final: The final or the acceptable configuration

Now we hope that the predicate logic is rich enough to describe these with logical formula. And we have two situations

Existence of a run: START ∧ TRANSITIONS ∧ FINAL is satisfiable

The run gives: START ∧ TRANSITIONS → FINAL is
valid

There are three different ways of making the predicate logic
rich enough

Using the term structure: The terms in predicate logic can
be used to simulate the words we need to describe computations

Using finite chains: We make the extra assumption that the
universe is a finite chain

Using the formal theory of a datastructure: We shall use
the datastructure of the binary trees

2.2 The language of words

Universe of words

An automaton does something with words — dissects a word
into individual symbols and does something with them. To describe automata we can use the language of words. Let us be
precise and look at words in a finite alphabet $\mathcal{A}$. The language
over $\mathcal{A}$ is a first order language where we have

- constantsymbol ε — the empty word

- one unary function symbol $\underline{a}$ for each symbol a from the alphabet $\mathcal{A}$ — $\underline{a}(x)$ gives the word where we have put the symbol a in front of the word x

- one binary relation symbol $\preceq$ where $u \preceq v$ means u is a prefix to v

In addition there may be more relation symbols. For example to describe automata below it is convenient to use some unary relation symbols. We shall come back to that when we come to applications.

Universe as a finite chain

Consider an individual word like

$$abba$$

We can think of this as given by a skeleton

$$0 - 1 - 2 - 3$$

where we color the skeleton with two colors

$$0 - 1 - 2 - 3$$

Such a skeleton is called a finite chain. It consists of a finite set which is totally ordered by a relation $<$ — think of it as a finite set of natural numbers ordered by $<$. A structure here is given by

---

Universe: The universe is a finite chain with total ordering $<$

Colorings: Two unary relations R and G which partitions the universe

Partitions: $\forall x(Rx \lor Gx) \land \neg \exists y(Ry \land Gy)$

Every such structure gives a word in the alphabet a and b — and conversely every word gives such a structure. It is straightforward to extend this to words in a finite alphabet. To describe automata this is interesting. We can think of a finite automaton as a coloring device. First we have the coloring of the skeleton which gives the words. But furthermore we can think of the states as a new set of colors. The start gives a state color for the first element, the transitions show how the state colors propagate along the skeleton and we get acceptance if we have an accepting color at the end.

Universe as set of binary trees

In programming we have learnt of the use of data structures to represent pieces of information and the syntactical transformation of the pieces. We consider here the data structure of binary trees. The signature is given by

$$\text{nil} : \mathcal{U}$$

cons $: \mathcal{U} \times \mathcal{U} \to \mathcal{U}$

$\prec : \mathcal{U} \times \mathcal{U} \to$ **Boole**

Here **nil** is intended to be the empty tree. We use **cons** to construct a new tree from two old ones. And $\prec$ is the subtree relation — in the datastructure $x \prec y$ means that x is constructed before y. This data structure is used to get lists in languages like Lisp, Haskell or Prolog, and is an ideal data structure to represent syntax. We show how to define a number of useful notions

$$
\begin{array}{lcl}
x \preceq y & : & x \prec y \vee x = y \\
\forall x \prec y.Fx & : & \forall x(x \prec y \to Fx) \\
\exists x \prec y.Fx & : & \exists x(x \prec y \wedge Fx) \\
\forall x \preceq y.Fx & : & Fy \wedge \forall x \prec y.Fx \\
\exists x \preceq y.Fx & : & Fy \vee \exists x \prec y.Fx \\
x = \mathbf{hd}(y) & : & \exists z \prec y.y = \mathbf{cons}(x, z) \\
x = \mathbf{tl}(y) & : & \exists z \prec y.y = \mathbf{cons}(z, x) \\
x \prec \mathbf{hd}(y) & : & \exists u \prec y.\exists v \prec y.(y = \mathbf{cons}(u, v) \wedge x \preceq v) \\
x \prec \mathbf{tl}(y) & : & \exists u \prec y.\exists v \prec y.(y = \mathbf{cons}(u, v) \wedge x \preceq u) \\
x \preceq \mathbf{hd}(y) & : & x = \mathbf{hd}(y) \vee x \prec \mathbf{hd}(y) \\
x \preceq \mathbf{tl}(y) & : & x = \mathbf{tl}(y) \vee x \prec \mathbf{tl}(y) \\
x = \mathbf{hd^*}(y) & : & x \preceq y \wedge \forall z \preceq y(x \prec z \to x \preceq \mathbf{hd}(z)) \\
x = \mathbf{tl^*}(y) & : & x \preceq y \wedge \forall z \preceq y(x \prec z \to x \preceq \mathbf{tl}(z))
\end{array}
$$

We have the usual definition of head and tail of a pair. The two important notions are

- the use of bounded quantifiers $\forall x \prec y$ and $\exists x \prec y$. We can think of them as sort of immediate between connectives and quantifiers. The idea is that we bound the quantifiers by terms from the datastructure — and the quantifiers will then run over some well controlled finite sets.

- we can define the arbitrary iteration of head or tail using only bounded quantifiers

2.3   Description — using the term structure

Take as an example an NFA where we search for subwords of the form *abba*. The automaton is

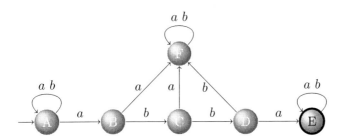

We have 6 states — A B C D E F . The alphabet is $\{a, b\}$. To transform the automaton to a first order framework we must decide on

Intended domain: Our elements are words in the alphabet

Configurations: The configurations are instantaneous descriptions of the run in the automaton. We can think of it as what we must remember if we stop the computation and would like to resume at some later time. The configurations are given by the state we are in and the part of the input word we have not used so far. We can represent it in first order logic by an atomic sentence $A(w)$ where A is a unary relation symbol giving the state and w is the remaining part of the word.

Signature: For our automaton above we have the following signature

- 6 unary relation symbols called A B C D E F — one for each of the states

- 1 constant symbol ε — for the empty word

- 2 function symbols $\underline{a}$ $\underline{b}$ — one for each element in the alphabet

In this language we can now write down a description of a run of the inputword w on the automaton

$$START(w) \wedge TRANSITIONS \rightarrow FINAL$$

where

START(w): $A(\underline{w})$

TRANSITIONS :

$$\forall x.(A(\underline{a}x) \to A(x)) \land$$
$$\forall x.(A(\underline{b}x) \to A(x)) \land$$
$$\forall x.(A(\underline{a}x) \to B(x)) \land$$
$$\forall x.(B(\underline{a}x) \to F(x)) \land$$
$$\forall x.(B(\underline{b}x) \to C(x)) \land$$
$$\forall x.(C(\underline{a}x) \to F(x)) \land$$
$$\forall x.(C(\underline{b}x) \to D(x)) \land$$
$$\forall x.(D(\underline{a}x) \to E(x)) \land$$
$$\forall x.(D(\underline{b}x) \to F(x)) \land$$
$$\forall x.(E(\underline{a}x) \to E(x)) \land$$
$$\forall x.(E(\underline{b}x) \to E(x)) \land$$
$$\forall x.(F(\underline{a}x) \to F(x)) \land$$
$$\forall x.(F(\underline{a}x) \to F(x))$$

FINAL : $E(\varepsilon)$

Some simple remarks on this construction

- To each word w correspond a term $\underline{w}$ which is the one we use above. For example to the word *abbabb* correspond the term $\underline{abbabb}\varepsilon$ written without parenthesis or more clumsily with parenthesis as $\underline{a}(\underline{b}(\underline{b}(\underline{a}(\underline{b}(\underline{b}(\varepsilon))))))$

- In TRANSITIONS we have a long conjunction of universally quantified formulas. There is one conjunct for each arrow in the transition diagram for the automaton.

- If we had more than one final state we get a disjunction of each of the states in FINAL.

This first order representation represents the run of the automaton in a faithfully way

Theorem 2.1 *If a word w is accepted, then*

$$START(w) \wedge TRANSITIONS \to FINAL$$

is provable.

We can just let the proof follow the same steps as the run of the automaton.

Theorem 2.2 *If a word w is not accepted, then*

$$START(w) \wedge TRANSITIONS \to FINAL$$

can be falsified.

Assume the w is not accepted. As a falsification model we take as domain the set of all words and interpret the constant symbol and the unary function symbols in the obvious way. We must tell how the atomic sentences are interpreted. Assume w can be written as $w = uv$ and after having gone through the u symbols of w we end up with state H, then we interpret $H(v)$

as true. All other atomic sentences are interpreted as false. We then see that $START(w)$ is true and TRANSITIONS is true. But since w is not accepted, then FINAL is false and the whole sentence is false.

We have gone through the simulations of automata within first order logic using an example. It should be clear that the constructions and the arguments are general. They can also be transferred to PDA's. In a PDA the configurations are a little more complicated. We must remember three things

- The state we are in

- The remainder of the input word

- The word on the stack

So the atomic sentences should be like $A(u, v)$ where A indicates the state, u the remainder of the input and v the stack. To simulate a PDA we use predicates with two arguments. It is straightforward how to write down the formula $START(w) \land TRANSITIONS \rightarrow FINAL$ also in this case.

2.4   Description — finite chain

We are now ready to use the chain structures to describe the computations in the automaton above. As a start we have the structure as given by

> **Universe:** The universe is a finite chain with total ordering $<$
>
> **Colorings:** Two unary relations R and G which partitions the universe
>
> **Partitions:** $\forall x.(Rx \vee Gx)$ and $\neg \exists y.(Ry \wedge Gy)$

Then we have the following statement

$\exists A. \exists B. \exists C. \exists D. \exists E. \exists F.$
$(Partition(A, B, C, D, E, F) \wedge Start \wedge Transition \wedge Final)$

where

Partition: Expresses that the unary relations A, B, C, D, E, F partitions the universe

Start: A is true for the first element in the chain

Transition: Gives the transitions between one element in the chain and the next element

Final: E is true for the last element in the chain

We can express "first", "next", "last" using the ordering $<$ of the finite chain.

We have got a sentence W in second order monadic logic over finite chains such that the structures which satisfies the sentence gives exactly the words accepted by the NFA. It is also possible to go the other way. Given any sentence U in second order monadic logic over finite chains we can find a DFA accepting exactly those words which satisfies U. But this leads us away from the path followed here.

2.5 Description — binary trees

The binary trees are given by

$$
\begin{array}{l}
\mathbf{nil} : \mathcal{U} \\[1ex]
\mathbf{cons} : \mathcal{U} \times \mathcal{U} \to \mathcal{U} \\[1ex]
\prec : \mathcal{U} \times \mathcal{U} \to \mathbf{Boole}
\end{array}
$$

Here **nil** is a constant and **cons** is the constructor used to build the datastructure. We have also the relation $x \prec y$ used to express that x is constructed before y — in this case that x is a subtree of y. We have seen that we can define new notions like head and tail, **hd** and **tl**, and especially iterated head and tail, **hd*** and **tl***. This is exactly what we need to define all kind of syntactical notions.

Let us be a little more concrete. We start with a finite set of trees representing information pieces. Here is what could have been an example

Such information pieces can be joined to get pair of information

The interesting constructions start when we can have an arbitrary number of information pieces

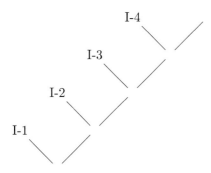

That a subtree x represents an information piece of y can then be written as

$$x = \mathbf{hd}\ \mathbf{tl^*}y$$

and this relation is defined by a formula with only bounded quantifiers. To represent some of the key syntactical notions — like being a proof or being a computation — we only need bounded quantifiers in the datastructure of binary trees. It turns out not to be so in the data structure of unary numbers. We define some classes of formulas

Δ_0: Can be defined using only connectives and bounded quantifiers

Π_1: Can be defined as $\forall x.Fx$ where Fx is Δ_0

Σ_1: Can be defined as $\exists x.Gx$ where Gx is Δ_0

Π_{n+1}: Can be defined as $\forall x.Kx$ where Kx is Σ_n

Σ_{n+1}: Can be defined as $\exists x.Lx$ where Lx is Π_n

Some concepts are naturally described using these classes

Syntactical: Properties described by Δ_0-formulas

Computable: Described by Σ_1-formula. There is a run satisfying some syntactical properties.

Invariant: For all input some syntactical properties holds.

Specification: For all input there is an output satisfying some syntactical relation.

Boundedness: There is a bound such that no matter which input some syntactical property holds.

We note that provability is also defined by a Σ_1-property.

2.6   Static descriptions — data bases

The descriptions of the runs of automata lead us up to the theory of data bases.

Database — logical point of view

Database: A finite structure over a signature over one or more universes

Query: A formula in the signature with one or more free variables

---

Example — company database

For the signature we have

Universe: The set of employers

Binary relation $\mathcal{R}$: $\mathcal{R}(x, y)$ means x reports to y

Then we can query the database about

- managers — $M(x) = \exists y.\mathcal{R}(y, x)$

- manager's manager — $K(x, y) = \exists z.(\mathcal{R}(x, z) \wedge \mathcal{R}(z, y))$

- manager's manager's manager — $L(x, y) = \exists z.\exists u.(\mathcal{R}(x, z) \wedge \mathcal{R}(z, u) \wedge \mathcal{R}(u, y))$

Some queries cannot be made within this framework. An example is to ask whether x and y are connected in such a chain where we have arbitrary many steps.

Example — university courses

For the signature we use three universes — teachers, courses and students — with variables and terms in three different colors

Blue universe: Teachers

Green universe: Courses

Red universe: Students

Ternary relation $\mathcal{S}(x, y, z)$: x teaches y to z

2.7 Dynamic description — abstract state machine

A computation can be given by

- Start

- Transitions

- Final

which tells us how the configurations are changed from step to step. The following is crucial

- The configurations are finite structures in a fixed signature

This was so in our three ways of describing computations with automata, and we used the signature to give the query language for the databases. In abstract state machines we start with the signature and the configurations as finite structures in the signature. The transition rules are then of the usual form

If guard, then action

where

Guard: Some formula which may or not be satisfied in a configuration

Action: Updating a configuration $f(t_1, \ldots, t_n) := g(u_1, \ldots, u_m)$

Simple examples of abstract state machines are turing machines as introduced in the next chapter.

Computations

3.1 Turings analysis

Alan Turing analyzed what it means for a (human) computer to follow an algorithm. The turing man sat down with a piece of paper and did his computation. He did this writing symbols on a squared paper. Consider the following multiplication

$$
\begin{array}{ccccc}
  &   & 3 & 7 & 8 \\
  &   & 1 & 2 & 3 \\
\hline
  & 1 & 1 & 3 & 4 \\
  & 7 & 5 & 6 &   \\
3 & 7 & 8 &   &   \\
\hline
4 & 6 & 4 & 9 & 4 \\
\end{array}
$$

We get the following

Computational medium: We do the computation on paper. The paper is divided into small squares — each square contains a symbol. The paper is unbounded, but only a bounded part contains non-blank symbols.

Active squares: When I do the computation I use say 3-4 active squares. These are the squares which I try to concentrate on.

Turing made the following simplification

- We can assume that the paper is 1-dimensional — a tape divided into squares

- Only one square is active

- In a square we can read its symbol and write a new symbol (erase the old symbol and write a new symbol above it)

- The computation is controlled by a finite state machine - with a start state and a halting state. The transitions are given by guards and actions. As guard we read symbol in active square. Actions we write a symbol in the active square and change the active square by L (move one step left), R (move one step right) and change the state. The controller is deterministic — there is at most one possible transition. If there are no transitions or we are in the halting state, then the turing machine halts.

- We start with a tape where a finite part may be written on and an active square.

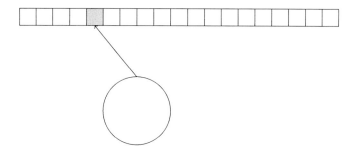

The main difference from a finite state automaton is that the active square can be moved in both directions.

3.2 Five basic machines

Basic 1: Producing a word

Say we have as alphabet *a b* and the blank 0 . The following machine produces the word *abba* on a blank tape and then stops

A word of length 4 is produced by a turing machine with 4 states. We assumed that we had a blank tape. But this does not matter.

Remember that a finite state automaton can be considered as a turing machine which moves only in one direction. This means that we can transfer the construction used for DFA's to turing machines — and can do things with words that can be described by regular expressions.

Basic 2: Changing a word

Say we want to run through a word built up from *a* and *b* and replacing the *b*'s with *a*'s and conversely. The word is limited by blanks on either side and we start to the left on the word. The following turing machine does it

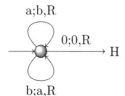

This machine is often used to clean up words after the computation. Again we see that we only run in one direction and are in the realm of finite state machines.

Basic 3 : Comparing a^m and b^n — right order

Given a tape of form $a^m b^n$. We want to compare the number of a's with the number of b's. We start on the first a to the left (or blank if there are no a's). We extend the alphabet with two new symbols A and B (for a and b treated). In addition we have as always the blank 0. Then

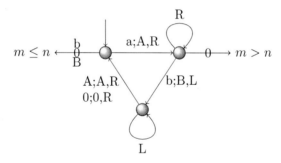

The problem goes beyond what we do with finite state machines. We have seen we need something like a PDA. We observe that our machine moves in both directions. The movements are like this

We compare each of the two words from left to right. We start on the leftmost position of the left word, find the leftmost position on the right word, go to the next position on the left word and so on.

We have used two abbreviations in the turing machine

Continuing in one direction: Say we are in a state and wants to go to the right until we meet an a. Then we write

Going out an exit: Say we are in a state and then wants to continue with S if we meet a c or d.

$$\bigcirc \xrightarrow[d]{c} S$$

The following variant of the machine copies a word in the alphabet **a b**

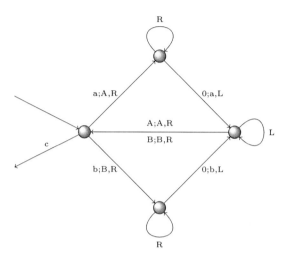

Exercise 3.1 *We consider turing machines where we have input tape using a and b and the blank symbol* 0.

1. *In basic 4 we ended up using also symbols A and B. Extend the machines such that we clean up the tape afterwards — replacing A with a and B with b.*

2. *Make a turing machine that compares two words in* $(a \lor b)^\star$.

3. *Make a turing machine that copies words in* $(a \lor b)^\star$.

4. *Make a turing machine that find out whether a word is a subword of another.*

If a question is imprecise or ambiguous you must make your own interpretation and tell what you have decided on. Have you remembered to clean up the tape afterwards ?

Basic 4 : Comparing a^m and b^n — inverse order

We start on the leftmost b and the tape head moves as follows

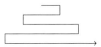

This procedure is faster — the tape head moves a shorter distance. And the turing machine is slightly simpler. But we compare the two words in different order which may cause a problem.

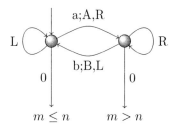

Exercise 3.2   *1. Compare two words in $(a \vee b)^\star$ using a variant of basic 4.*

2. Explain the difference between comparing words in right or in inverse order when the alphabet is larger than 1.

3. Use basic 4 to make a copyer.

Basic 5 : Converting binary to unary

Let b be the blank symbol. The start tape is a binary number $(0 \vee 1)^*$ with head to the rightmost symbol. The final tape is $1^* x^*$ where we have as many x's as given by the binary number. The number of 1's is the number of bits in the binary number. The machine is

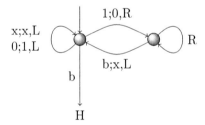

We convert in a loop where we subtract 1 from the binary number and add an x to the unary. Observe how we subtract 1. We start in the binary number to the right. Then we go left changing 0 to 1 until we meet 1 which we change to 0. We are finished when we do not meet 1.

Exercise 3.3 *1. Make a machine which converts unary to binary.*

2. Make a machine which converts decimal to unary.

3. Make a machine which converts between numbers in binary and 3-number system (Numbers written in base 3).

4. We have a long sequence of words in a ∨ b separated by an x. Find a machine which to a number n in binary notation find word number n in the sequence.

3.3   Universal machine

Turings analysis

Say we want to study a human doing multiplication following one of the usual algorithms. Now there are a number of simplifications

Computational medium: We would usually perform the multiplication on a piece of paper and the computation organised in a 2-dimensional array. Using some more steps we can do the multiplication on a 1-dimensional tape divided up into squares. There is no limitation on the number of squares on the tape even if we only use a finite part of it for each concrete multiplication.

Symbols: There is a finite alphabet of symbols used. For the multiplication we may use the 10 digits and the blank symbol.

States: There is a finite number of states given by the algorithm. We can think of this as the number of distinctions
that the human computer must remember during the computation.

Scanned square: We only scan one square at a time. For the
multiplication we may often use 3-4 squares — 2 for digits
from each factor and 1-2 for where the resulting digit is
written. Using more states in describing the algorithm we
can do with only 1 scanned square.

Configuration: Each moment in a computation is described
by the finite number of non-blank symbols on the tape,
the scanned square and the state.

Transitions: We describe the algorithm using a transition
table. Each transition is given by a guard (symbol in
scanned square, state) and an action (next symbol in scanned
square, next state, movement left or right to a neighboring
square as the next scanned square). The transitions are
deterministic – they tell you how to get from one configuration to the next.

Computational run: Each computation starts with a start
configuration and using the transitions we get to the next
configurations. The computation terminates if it comes to
a halting state.

Variants – Machine with two registers

Turings analysis is robust. There are a number of changes which could be made without changing the functions which could be computed

- We could have used more tapes and could have tapes with other geometrical shapes than a 1-dimensional array.

- It is only necessary to have the tape infinite in only one direction.

- We could have more than 1 scanned square.

These changes may affect the number of steps required for a concrete computation, but they do not change which functions are computable.

An interesting way of looking at a turing machine is as a PDA with 2 stacks. Given a turing machine with a tape where we have painted the left and the right of the scanned square as follows

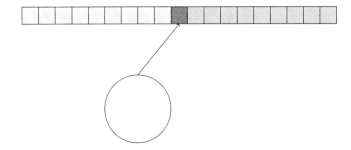

Now break this up into two stacks and get

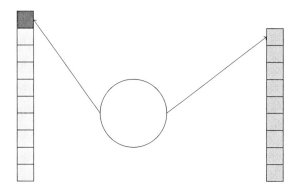

The usual tape operations can be transferred to operations on the two stacks. The two stacks contains each a word in the alphabet. Imagine that we have just the binary alphabet — 1 and the blank symbol 0. Then each stack can be seen as a number given in binary notation. The whole computation can be represented as a computation on two registers — each containing a number. And the stack operations has simple interpretations

Push 0:   Doubling a number — $2m$

Push 1:   Doubling and add $1 - 2m + 1$

Pop :   Taking half of a number — $\lceil m/2 \rceil$

Top? :   Test whether the number is odd or even

A machine with 2 registers for numbers where we can double, take half and investigate parity can do the same thing as a turing machine.

Variants — problems with tiles

Consider a computation of a turing machine. Now put the tapes for the various steps under each other so we get a large 2-dimensional array where each horisontal row is the instance of the tape at some moment.

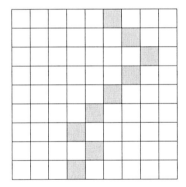

Here we have indicated with gray the scanned square. We see that it moves at most one place at each step. The interesting observation is that the only change from one step to the next is in the square scanned and its 2 neighbor squares. All the other squares are not changed. We can translate the problems with computations on a turing machine to problems with tiling a room. The tiles are oriented and all of the following form

with an indication of which sides are up, down, left, right. The rooms are now tiled such that we always have matching colors against each other. Say now that we have a turing machine with alphabet of size m and with n states. We then use $1 + m + n + mn$ colors and $m + 3mn$ types of tiles. Below we have indicated the color white and the other colors with a symbol — either symbol from the alphabet or state or a pair from alphabet and state

For each a from the alphabet:

For each transition (b,p;c,q,R):

For each transition (b,p;c,q,L):

For each b from alphabet and q from state:

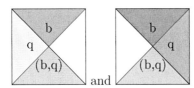
and

We have 1 white color, m colors from the alphabet and mn colors giving pairs from the alphabet and the state. The pairs indicate where the scanned square is.

There is an extra problem with how to start and stop the turing machine. We leave that to the reader. But it is clear that the problem of putting down the tiles in a correct way is the same as doing a computation on the turing machine.

Constructing the universal machine

One of Turings fundamental insights is the following

> The operations of a turing machine consists of simple book keeping operations like find, replace, copy, ... They are so simple that we can let a turing machine do them.

In an ordinary turing machine we have

The machine can be represented as a table of transitions and the architecture of the universal machine is

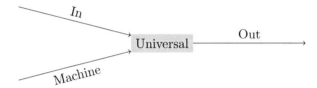

3.4 Halting problem is undecidable

We shall give a short proof by contradiction that we cannot decide whether turing machines halt or not. Assume that there is a turing machine HALTING which solves the halting problem. As input we have DATA and PROGRAM and there are two possible outputs — YES and NO — for the machine PROGRAM starting on DATA halts and for the machine PROGRAM on DATA does not halt.

Now we make two changes on the halting machine — at the start we have a copyer to duplicate the input and at the YES-exit we write a loop (making no termination)

We call this machine for $\mathcal{T}$. We then have

$$\mathcal{T} \text{ applied on } \mathcal{T} \text{ stops}$$
$$\Updownarrow$$
$$\text{The HALTING machine will exit in the upper exit}$$
$$\Updownarrow$$
$$\mathcal{T} \text{ applied on } \mathcal{T} \text{ does not stop}$$

So we have a contradiction — and there is no HALTING machine.

3.5   Busy beaver

Some beavers

Consider turing machines with alphabet $\{0, 1\}$ and 0 as the blank symbol. Assume we have a machine with N ordinary states and the halting state. We can estimate the number of such machines

- there are $2N$ guards

- each transition can perform $2(N + 1)2$ possible actions

So there are $(4N + 4)^{2N}$ possible turing machines with N ordinary states and 2 symbols. An N-beaver is such a turing machine which halts after having been started on a blank tape. Some of the $(4N + 4)^{2N}$ turing machines are N-beavers and others are not — they do not halt. Among the N-beavers there is at least one which is particularly busy — it is the one which produces most 1's before it stops. The busy beaver function $\beta(n)$ gives the maximal number of 1's which the n-beavers can produce.

Busy 1-beaver

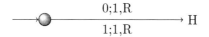

On a blank tape it only writes a 1 and stops. We have also put the arrow with $1; 1, R$ in for completeness, but this transition will not be used.

Busy 2-beaver

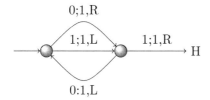

It produces 4 1's and stops after 6 steps.

Busy 3-beaver

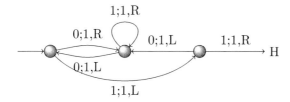

The machine stops after 13 steps with 6 1's on the tape. There is a 3-beaver which also produces 6 1's but stops after 21 steps — but the 6 1's is the maximal number.

Busy 4-beaver

It is possible to produce 13 1's with 4 states. It is the maximal number

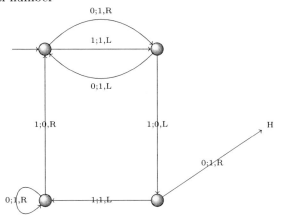

Other beavers

The value at 5 of the busy beaver function is not known in 2010. A candidate produces 4098 1's after 47176870 steps. For 6-beavers the record holder (2010) produces $3.5 \cdot 10^{18267}$ 1's.

Problem 3.4 *Find a very busy 4-beaver. And then try on a 5-beaver.*

The busy beaver function is not computable

We shall show that $\beta(n)$ grows faster than any function computable on a turing machine. Let $f(n)$ be a computable function. We can assume the following about the computation

- The computation is performed on a turing machine with k states and in the alphabet 0,1

- In the computation we start with a tape with n consecutive 1's

- The result of the computation is written as $f(n)$ consecutive 1's

- At the start and at the stop we are on the first blank to the left of the consecutive 1's and except for the consecutive 1's everything else is blank.

It is sufficient to consider functions $f(n)$ which are such that

- $f(n) \geq n^2$ — f grows faster than any linear function

- $f(n+1) > f(n)$ — f is strictly increasing

If this was not the case we could replace $f(n)$ with $F(n) = \Sigma_{i \leq n}(i^2 + f(i))$ and then show that the beaver function grows faster than F.

We write $g \succ h$ for $\exists m.\forall n \geq m.g(n) > h(n)$. We say that g grows faster than h and means that g is larger than h for sufficiently large numbers. An example is that the square n^2

grows faster than any linear function. Now we want to show that the busy beaver function β grows faster than any such computable f. The crucial observation is

- Assume the function f can be computed with k states

- Then $f(f(n))$ can be computed with $2k$ states — just have a turing machine to compute $f(n)$ and let the same turing machine have this as input to produce $f(f(n))$

- We can find a beaver with $n + 2k$ states that produces the number $f(f(n))$ — from the blank tape we use first n states to produce n then k states to produce $f(n)$ and k more states to produce $f(f(n))$

But then

$$\beta(n + 2k) \geq f(f(n)) \geq f(n^2) \succ f(n + 2k)$$

and we are done. The Beaver function grows faster than any computable function. This gives another proof that the halting problem is undecidable.

3.6   Rice's theorem

By a non-trivial predicate we mean a predicate which is sometimes true and sometimes false.

Theorem 3.1 (Rice) *There are no non-trivial decidable extensional predicate.*

Proof. Assume we have a non-trivial extensional predicate $\mathcal{P}$ which is decidable.Consider the machine UNDEF which never stops. There are now two cases

- UNDEF satisfies $\mathcal{P}$

- UNDEF does not satisfy $\mathcal{P}$

The two cases are similar. In both cases we shall show that we could make a procedure which would decide whether a program started on blank tape stops — and get a contradiction. We give the details for the first case. Assume UNDEF satisfies $\mathcal{P}$ and that we have another program Q which does not satisfy $\mathcal{P}$.

Let R be any program. Then construct a new program by

1. Store the input for Q

2. Start R on blank tape

3. If R stops, then start with Q on its stored input

4. If R does not stop, then just continue

The program is either extensionally equal to Q or extensionally equal to UNDEF. It is extensionally equal to Q if and only if R stops on blank tape. Hence using the predicate $\mathcal{P}$ we can decide whether the program R stops on blank tape. This is impossible in general. There is no such decidable predicate $\mathcal{P}$.

The details for the second case — UNDEF does not satisfy $\mathcal{P}$ — is similar and is left to the reader. ∎

Rice's theorem gives a nice way of arguing that extensional properties are undecidable. Consider the property that a machine halts. This is an extensional property — it only concerns the INPUT/OUTPUT relation. Now there is a machine which halts and another one which does not. So the halting problem is undecidable.

Logic 4

4.1 Logic as language

We assume that you already know the language of first order logic. For repetition we list some of the important elements

Connectives: **Verum:** $\top$
    Falsum: $\bot$
    Negation: $\neg$
    Conjunction: $\wedge$
    Disjunction: $\vee$
    Conditional: $\rightarrow$
    Inverse conditional: $\leftarrow$
    Biconditional: $\leftrightarrow$

Quantifiers: **Universal:** $\forall$
    Existential: $\exists$

Free and bound variables: A variable is bound if it is within the scope of a quantifier

Signature: Giving constant symbols, function symbols and relation symbols

Formulas, literals and sentences: Formulas are built up from atomic formulas using connectives and quantifiers. Literals are either atomic formulas or negation of atomic formulas. Sentences are formulas without free variables.

In first order logic the variables range over individuals. We used second order language in describing automata. There we had variables ranging over unary relations. We could also have other variables — but we are not going to explore this further here.

4.2 Sequent calculus

We list some of the equivalences in logic

$$
\begin{aligned}
A \leftrightarrow B &\Leftrightarrow (A \to B) \wedge (A \leftarrow B) \\
A \leftarrow B &\Leftrightarrow \quad\quad B \to A \\
A \to B &\Leftrightarrow \quad\quad \neg A \vee B \\
\bot &\Leftrightarrow \quad\quad A \wedge \neg A \\
\top &\Leftrightarrow \quad\quad A \vee \neg A
\end{aligned}
$$

Using these we can replace formulas in our language with formulas built up from $\neg \ \wedge \ \vee \ \forall \ \exists$.

We can also use de Morgans laws to push negation in front of the atomic formulas

$$
\begin{aligned}
\neg(A \vee B) &\Leftrightarrow \neg A \wedge \neg B \\
\neg(A \wedge B) &\Leftrightarrow \neg A \vee \neg B \\
\neg \forall x.Fx &\Leftrightarrow \exists x.\neg Fx \\
\neg \exists x.Fx &\Leftrightarrow \forall x.\neg Fx \\
\neg\neg A &\Leftrightarrow \quad A
\end{aligned}
$$

In this way we get formulas built up from literals using $\wedge \ \vee \ \forall \ \exists$. Such formulas are said to be in negation normal form.

Propositional logic

We consider sentences built up by $\wedge$ $\vee$ from literals. It is straight-forward to have a calculus for such formulas. We just use the same construction as with alternating automata — we start with a sentence and then build a tree above it. We analyze disjunction using conjunctive nodes and conjunctions using disjunctive nodes. The leafnodes of the trees contain literals. In the alternating automata we can get rid of the conjunctive nodes using a subset construction. We do the same here and we get the sequent calculus. The resulting calculus has the following ingredients

Sequents: Finite set of formulas — usually written as Γ or Δ. We also write Γ, F for $\Gamma \cup \{F\}$ and F for $\{F\}$

Rule for $\wedge$:

$$\frac{\Gamma, F \quad \Gamma, G}{\Gamma, F \wedge G}$$

Rule for $\vee$:

$$\frac{\Gamma, F, G}{\Gamma, F \vee G}$$

Axiom: A sequent which both contains a literal and its negation

First order logic

It is not surprising that we can make a calculus for propositional logic. Such a calculus has been found independently by a number of people. It is more surprising that a calculus can be found for first order logic. This was done by Thoralf Skolem in 1922 constructing the calculus and showing completeness. We extend the calculus for propositional logic with two rules

Rule for ∀:

$$\frac{\Gamma, Fa}{\Gamma, \forall x.Fx}$$

Here a is a new variable — it does not occur in $\Gamma, \forall x.Fx$

Rule for ∃:

$$\frac{\Gamma, Ft, \exists x.Fx}{\Gamma, \exists x.Fx}$$

Here t is a term

Two-sided sequent calculus

We simplified the development of sequent calculus by first translating formulas into negation normal form and then making the calculus with such formulas. In two sided sequent calculus we make the rules and the sequents directly for all formulas. A sequent will then look like

$$\Gamma \vdash \Delta$$

where Γ is called the *antecedent* and Δ the *succedent*.

In the analysis interpretation we try to falsify the sequent by having a model where all formulas in Γ are true and all formulas in Δ are false. In the synthesis interpretation we try to make the formula

$$G_1 \wedge \ldots \wedge G_m \to D_1 \vee \ldots \vee D_n$$

valid. Here the G's are the formulas in Γ and the D's are the formulas in Δ. From this it is not too hard to write down the rules. Note that we have two sets of rules for each connective and quantifier. The axioms are

$$\Gamma, A \vdash \Delta, A$$

where A is atomic. We give the rules for negation, conjunction, disjunction and conditional:

	antecedent	succedent
$\neg$	$\dfrac{\Gamma \vdash \Delta, F}{\Gamma, \neg F \vdash \Delta}$	$\dfrac{\Gamma, F \vdash \Delta}{\Gamma \vdash \Delta, \neg F}$
$\wedge$	$\dfrac{\Gamma, F, G \vdash \Delta}{\Gamma, F \wedge G \vdash \Delta}$	$\dfrac{\Gamma \vdash \Delta, F \quad \Gamma \vdash \Delta, G}{\Gamma \vdash \Delta, F \wedge G}$
$\vee$	$\dfrac{\Gamma, F \vdash \Delta \quad \Gamma, G \vdash \Delta}{\Gamma, F \vee G \vdash \Delta}$	$\dfrac{\Gamma \vdash \Delta, F, G}{\Gamma \vdash \Delta, F \vee G}$
$\rightarrow$	$\dfrac{\Gamma \vdash \Delta, F \quad \Gamma, G \vdash \Delta}{\Gamma, F \rightarrow G \vdash \Delta}$	$\dfrac{\Gamma, F \vdash \Delta, G}{\Gamma \vdash \Delta, F \rightarrow G}$

Exercise 4.1 *Write down the two-sided rules for the other connectives and the quantifiers.*

The remainder of the theory below is easily translated to the two-sided sequent calculus. One advantage with the two-sided sequent calculus is that we can use it to give formal systems for other logics. We shall not go further into this here.

4.3 Analysis and synthesis

There are two main interpretations of the rules — the analysis interpretation looks at the rules upwards and the synthesis interpretation looks at the rules downwards. The analysis stresses falsifications and the synthesis stresses validity. For sequents we say that a sequent is falsified there is a falsification of all its elements simultaneously. A sequent is valid if in each interpretation one of its elements are true. So for falsification we have conjunction of the elements in the sequent, and for validity we have disjunction of the elements.

The analysis interpretation

We try to systematically falsify the sequents by falsifying simultaneously all formulas in the sequent. Let us look at each rule

Conjunction: We falsify the sequent $\Gamma, F \wedge G$ by either falsifying Γ, F or by falsifying Γ, G. The branching is taken disjunctively.

Disjunction: We falsify the sequent $\Gamma, F \vee G$ by falsifying Γ, F, G.

Universal quantification: We falsify $\Gamma, \forall x.Fx$ by introducing a new parameter a and falsifying Γ, Fa. The parameter a is a name for a falsifying instance of $\forall x.Fx$. We have no guarantee that we already have a name for a falsifying instance and we are safe to introduce a new name — either for some element we know already or some new element we have not seen before.

Existential quantification: We falsify $\Gamma, \exists x.Fx$ by falsifying $\Gamma, \exists x.Fx, Ft$. The problem here is that we must falsify Ft for all names t for elements — both names that we know already and names which we shall introduce later. This rule may give rise to an infinite process and we must watch the rule carefully.

Axiom: An axiom contains both a literal and its negation —
and cannot therefore be falsified.

The synthesis interpretation

We now look at the rules downwards and consider the disjunction of the formulas in the sequents. We start with the
axioms and show that for all sequents their disjunctions are
valid.

Axiom: An axiom contains both a literal and its negation —
so it is valid as a sequent.

Conjunction: Assume both Γ, F and Γ, G are valid. Then
so is $\Gamma, F \wedge G$. Note that the branching in the synthesis
interpretation is taken conjunctively.

Disjunction: Assume Γ, F, G is valid. Then so is $\Gamma, F \vee G$.

Universal quantification: Assume Γ, Fa is valid where the
parameter a does not occur in the conclusion. Then so is
$\Gamma, \forall x.Fx$.

Existential quantification: Assume $\Gamma, \exists x.Fx, Ft$ is valid. Then
so is $\Gamma, \exists x.Fx$.

Infinite processes

If we try to analyze a formula $\exists x.\forall y.F(x, y)$ we may get an
infinite process

$$
\begin{array}{c}
\cdots\cdots \\
\hline
\exists x.\forall y.F(x,y), \forall y.F(c,y), F(a,b), F(b,c) \\
\hline
\exists x.\forall y.F(x,y), F(a,b), F(b,c) \\
\hline
\exists x.\forall y.F(x,y), \forall y.F(b,y), F(a,b) \\
\hline
\exists x.\forall y.F(x,y), F(a,b) \\
\hline
\exists x.\forall y.F(x,y), \forall y.F(a,y) \\
\hline
\exists x.\forall y.F(x,y)
\end{array}
$$

We may even get an infinite process if we analyze $\exists x.G(x)$ and the language contains a function symbol. Then there are infinitely many terms we may substitute for x.

But we know of some of the pitfalls of infinite processes. We must be careful that the processes are fair — in the analysis everything that can be analyzed should be sooner or later analyzed.

4.4 Completeness

In this section we shall show that our calculus captures exactly all valid sentences. There are four main ingredients in the proof:

1. The rules propagates falsifications upwards — the analysis interpretation

The rules are such that if a premiss is falsified, then at least one of the premisses is falsified. We can use the same falsification in the conclusion as we do in the premiss. This is straightforward for most of the rules. Observe how it is done for the analysis of ∀.

2. The rules propagates validity downwards — the synthesis interpretation

This is also obvious by inspection.

3. We can always produce a fully analyzed analysis tree over a sequent

Given a sequent Γ we use the rules to produce an analysis tree over Γ. We can always assume that the analysistree is fair and fully analyzed. This means that along each branch in the tree if there is a formula which could be analyzed (with respect to some term in the branch), then sooner or later it will be analyzed. We use standard techniques to produce such a fair process.

4. A fully analyzed branch without axioms in an analysis tree over Γ gives a falsification of Γ

As universe we take the set of all terms occurring in the branch. The interpretation is defined such that it gives a falsification to all literals in the branch. Since the branch does not contain any axiom, then this is a proper interpretation. By induction over the build up of formulas we get all formulas in the branch falsified in this interpretation.

Theorem 4.1 (Completeness) *For any sequent Γ: Γ is derivable if and only if it is valid.*

Proof. If – part. Assume Γ is not derivable. We produce a fully analysed analysis tree over Γ. It contains a branch with no axioms, and this branch gives a falsification of Γ. So Γ is not valid.

Only if – part. Assume Γ is not valid, but derivable. Consider the derivability tree over Γ. The falsification of Γ propagates upwards, and gives a branch where all sequents are falsified. This branch does not contain any axiom, and we did not have a derivability tree. ∎

4.5 Equality

We can use equality as a logical symbol. We then extend the system with an extra axiom and an extra rule

Equality axiom: $\Gamma, s = s$ for any term s

Equality rule: For literals F

$$\frac{\Gamma, F, F^\star, \neg s = t}{\Gamma, F, \neg s = t}$$

where $F^\star$ is obtained from F by substituting some s for t and some t for s

The completeness goes through for first order logic with equality. The only change from the above is in the construction of the falsification from a fully analyzed branch without axioms. We observe that the equality relation is an equivalence relation between terms and in the falsification model we let the universe be the equivalence classes of the terms.

4.6 Variants

Many sorted logic

This is an obvious and useful extension of our logic. We usually extend the language with variables for each sort and in the interpretation we have one universe for each sort. It is a straightforward exercise to make such a logic — we are just careful that the completeness argument will still go through.

Higher order logic

One way to look at it is as a two sorted language

- one sort for elements

- another sort for say unary relations

- one relation between the two sorts — an element satisfies a relation

Then we can make more or less strict requirements on the relation sort. The strictest is that the universe of relations should contain all relations over the universe of elements. The loosest requirement is that we have no extra requirement.

Finite logic (finite model theory)

In finite model theory we require that the universe is a finite chain. Here we open up for a number of other possibilities and a number of new logics.

Constructive or intuitionistic logic

Perhaps the main connective in logic is the conditional $A \to B$. In classical logic we interpret this as the same as $\neg A \vee B$. This is sufficient to use the conditional in the simulation of computations. This is perhaps the main test that the conditional works as it should. In constructive logic there is another interpretation of the conditional. We interpret $A \to B$ as "There exists a function which to a proof of A gives a proof of B". Instead of function we could have used rule, method, construction, ... We often use the name intuitionistic logic instead of constructive logic.

Indeterminacy and vagueness

In Jeff Paris: "The uncertain reasoner's companion" there is a survey of ways of interpreting indeterminacy or vagueness.

In favor of indeterminacy and vagueness

A logic where you consider indeterminacy and vagueness is often taken as more realistic than the usual classical logic — and there are a number of proposals for such logics. Jeff Paris mentions the use of probability, fuzzy logic and logics where one has an interval of truth values. All these have their advantages and disadvantages.

Against indeterminacy and vagueness

The main argument against a logic where we have indeterminacy and vagueness is that it is not able to simulate computations. Constructive logic and classical logic does it with no problems.

4.7   Logic for binary trees

In first order logic we have a calculus for derivability. This can be extended to formal systems where we investigate derivations from axioms. Let us do this for binary trees. As a first attempt we take as axioms all true syntactical sentences — we take all true Δ_0-sentences. Using alternating trees there are obvious procedures for finding out whether a Δ_0-sentence is true or false.

There is a drawback that there are infinitely many true Δ_0-sentences. One can use the following five sentences

1. $\forall x, y. \neg \mathbf{nil} = \mathbf{cons}(x, y)$

2. $\forall x, y, u, v.(\mathbf{cons}(x, y) = \mathbf{cons}(u, v) \rightarrow x = u \vee y = v)$

3. $\forall x.(x = \mathbf{nil} \vee \exists u, v.x = \mathbf{cons}(u, v))$

4. $\forall x. \neg x \prec \mathbf{nil}$

5. $\forall x, u, v. (x \prec \mathbf{cons}(u, v) \rightarrow x \preceq u \lor x \preceq v)$

Here we have used obvious abbreviations like $\forall x, y$ and $\preceq$. We write the conjunction of these sentences for $\mathcal{R}$. We can then investigate whether Γ is derivable in the formal system by investigating whether $\neg \mathcal{R}, \Gamma$ (or $\mathcal{R} \rightarrow \Gamma$) is derivable in first order logic with equality.

Using the axioms $\mathcal{R}$ we can derive all true Δ_0-sentences.

4.8 Incompleteness

There are two main ways of simulating a computation using derivability in first order logic:

Using terms for words: This was done for automata where we considered a single run. We can clearly use the same technique to simulate a computation on a turing machine using two words.

Using formal theory of a data structure: To get the syntactical transformation of the computation and the simulation of a run right it is sufficient to consider Δ_0-formulas over binary trees. As axioms we must have enough power to be able to derive all true Δ_0-sentences.

Now we know from the halting problem that there are no way to decide in general whether a computation halts. This gives the following results

Theorem 4.2 (Entscheidungsproblem) *There is no general way to decide whether a sequent in first order logic is derivable or not.*

Proof. If the sequent is derivable, then our procedure will find a derivation. But if it is not derivable (falsifiable), then there are no method which will find the falsification. If there were, we could use the method to decide the halting problem. ∎

Theorem 4.3 (Incompleteness) *There are no axiom system for binary trees which derives exactly those Π_1-sentences which are true. For each proposed axiom system which is consistent, there are true Π_1-sentences which are not derivable.*

Proof. All the reasonable axiom systems $\mathcal{A}$ for a datastructure derives exactly those Σ_1-sentences which are true. Assume we also had an axiom system $\mathcal{B}$ which did the same for the Π_1-sentences. Then observe that for any computation $\mathbf{c}$ we have

- $\mathbf{c}$ halts is a Σ_1 sentence

- $\mathbf{c}$ does not halt is a Π_1 sentence

But then we can use derivations in $\mathcal{A}$ and $\mathcal{B}$ to decide whether $\mathbf{c}$ halts or not. This is impossible and the theorem is proved. ∎

Complexity

5.1 Growth

In a computation we use resources — time, space, money, people, nature, ... Complexity theory wants to give estimates of the resources used as a function of the size of the input data. Here we concentrate on the resources of space and time. Space can be seen as the memory used, and time as the number of steps used. We get functions from numbers to numbers — and we are interested in how fast the functions grow.

Definition 5.1 *Given two functions $f, g : \mathcal{N} \to \mathcal{N}$.*

$$f \prec g \quad \Leftrightarrow \quad \forall x. \exists y > x. \forall z > y. f(z) < g(z)$$
$$f \preceq g \quad \Leftrightarrow \quad \forall x. \exists y > x. \forall z > y. f(z) \leq g(z)$$

We say that g grow faster than f when $f \preceq g$, and that g grow strictly faster than f when $f \prec g$.

So we disregard the start of the functions and are only interested in comparing the functions for large enough values.

Exercise 5.1 *Show*

1. $1000 \cdot N \prec N^2$

2. $N^2 \prec N^3$

3. $2 \cdot N^2 \prec 3 \cdot N^2$

4. $N^{1000} \prec 2^N$

91

So we get a hierarchy of faster and faster functions using the polynomials and then exponential functions. Often we want to disregard the the coefficients and want to say that $2 \cdot N^2$ and $3 \cdot N^2$ grows equally fast. We then introduce the O-notation.

Definition 5.2 $f = O(g)$ *whenever* $\exists M.f \preceq M \cdot g$.

We compare f with g multiplied by some constant. Using this we get

Exercise 5.2   *1.* $2 \cdot N^2 = O(3 \cdot N^2)$

2. $3 \cdot N^2 = O(2 \cdot N^2)$

3. For any two second order polynomials p and q, we have $p = O(q)$ and $q = O(p)$

5.2   Tiling a room

We have seen that to tile a room with a finite set of types of tiles is the same as doing a computation on a turing machine. Now we can describe the complexity measures using the tiles

Time: The number of steps the turing machine uses. This is the same as the number of rows in the tiling.

Space: The number of squares where non-blank is used. This is the same as the number of columns with non-blank tiles.

And then we have the complexity measures. Say that we have a computation where we start with DATA on the tape. Then a computation is

NP: Non deterministic polynomial time. The tiling is done in a square room where the sides are of length polynomial in DATA.

PSPACE: Polynomial space. The tiling is done in a corridor where the width is polynomial in DATA.

5.3   Computations in trees

There is an interesting and close connection between the complexity classes and the trees with disjunctive and conjunctive nodes which we have seen in our automata. We return to our basic situation

DATA ─────────────▸│MACHINE├─────────▸ YES/NO

We start with some DATA and then want to describe the use of space or time in our machine as a function of the size of the DATA.

From trees to tiles

Imagine that we can organize the computation in a tree. The computation on a deterministic turing machine is just a computation on a tree with no branchings at all. It goes like this

There are no choices, no decisions — we just go along a one-way street. So this is the picture of **P**. The length of the road is polynomial in the data.

Then we come to **NP**. Here we have decisions to make and the computations look like

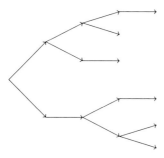

Some of the leaf nodes may be acceptable, others may not be. In the computation we search for an acceptable leaf node. If we try to check whether all leaf nodes are acceptable, then we are in the complementary complexity class **CO-NP** and treat the nodes as conjunctive. We would not do this search with a non-deterministic turing machine — they do not exist. Instead we would try a depth first search. This search uses little space. Observe now that the depth first search work equally well for

trees with both conjunctive and disjunctive nodes. So we could
have the following situation

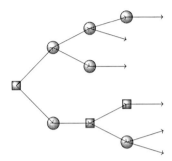

   Using this depth first search we see that the complexity of
the computation is **PSPACE** — at each stage we only had
to rememember the path back to the root and a little extra
decoration on the nodes.

From tiles to trees

   The correspondence is straightforward for **P** and **NP**. We
must show that a **PSPACE** computation can be organized with
a polynomial tree with conjunctive and disjunctive nodes. We
think of a **PSPACE** computation as tiling along a corridor

The width of the corridor is polynomial in DATA. We do not know the length of the corridor. But we know that the number of configurations is exponential in DATA. Say that it is

$$K^{\mathrm{DATA}}$$

The tiling can then be done in conjunctive and disjunctive phases as follows

Disjunctive phase: Chose $K - 1$ intermediate configurations $A, B, C, \ldots, M$

Conjunctive phase: Show that we can tile from start to A, from A to B, . . . and from M to the final configuration

Traversing the tree: This can be done in a polynomial way. Observe that the K^{DATA} disjunctions can be obtained by enumerating in a K-ary number system.

5.4   Logarithms and exponentials

There are two different sources for the exponentials as used in complexity theory

Change: If the rate of change of a population depends only on the size, we get an exponential growth.

Names: There are exponentially many things with names of a certain size.

In the former the rate of change is typically given as a constant multiple of the size and the size is given by a simple differential equation. In complexity theory we are especially interested in the exponentiation connected with names. So imagine that we have an alphabet of size K and use it to write names of length M. Then we can give names to K^M things. We have the following situation

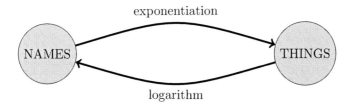

We can use binary trees to give names in the alphabet $\{l, r\}$. Each node corresponds to a word in the alphabet, and we have names of length N for the leaf nodes in the binary tree of height N. Below is the binary tree height 2 with names on the nodes

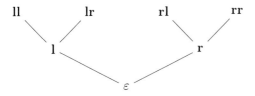

Taking logarithms does the inverse — it takes the number of things into an estimate of the length of names needed to name them.

A number of algorithms works on names for things and it is often natural that we get exponentiations and logarithms in estimating the complexity.

We have learned that the unary numbers is often an awful data structure to work with. The only way we get to a large number is to count from 0 and upwards. This can be extended using addition and multiplication. This is something which is easy to visualize:

Addition:

But then it stops. We must think of exponentiation as a process — we cannot count up to the estimated number of atoms in the universe

$$10^{80}$$

but as a number in the decimal notation it is just 80 digits and does not look so formidable. With the decimal notation we jump up one exponential. With the so called scientific notation we jump up two exponentials and consider numbers like

$$4.13 \cdot 10^{80}$$

But then two exponentials up we work just as we did with the unary numbers.

5.5   Notations

We are used to having a data structure and on the top of it having a language of notations.

Let us start with the unary numbers as given by:

- constant 0

- successor s

- function symbols

- predicate Nx — x is a number

- first order logic with equality

- axiom NUM — $N0 \land \forall x(Nx \to Nsx)$

The function symbols will be used later for defining notations. We define addition and multiplication by

$$
\begin{aligned}
+0y &= y \\
+sxy &= s + xy \\
*0y &= 0 \\
*sxy &= +y * xy
\end{aligned}
$$

Here we have used a Polish notation for addition and multiplication. A notation system is a set of equations. It is sound if
it can be interpreted in the natural numbers. It is complete if
we can derive all true atomic sentences.

A particularly interesting notation system is got from the
binary function symbol e and the equations $\mathcal{E}$

$$
\begin{aligned}
e0y &= sy \\
esxy &= exexy
\end{aligned}
$$

We interpret exy as $2^x + y$ and observe that $\mathcal{E}$ is sound and
complete.

Using terms built up from e, s and 0 we can make short
notations for some very large numbers. The number

$$
eeeeee0000000 = 2^{2^{16}}
$$

is a number much larger than the number of atoms in the
universe.

We have three ingredients:

Datastructure: Here we have the data structure of unary numbers

Language: We use sound and complete equations to define new functions. They can be used to define terms which are denoting unary numbers. In this way we get names for some large numbers.

Calculus: We use the calculus of first order logic with equality to derive properties of the new notations.

Assume we have a term t built up by function symbols defined by equations $\mathcal{R}$. The simplest property is to investigate whether we can build up t from below. This amounts to deriving

$$\text{NUM} \wedge \mathcal{R} \to Nt$$

Let us see how our calculus treats a problem like this. We know that if it is valid, then our calculus will give a derivation. But there is no guarantee that the derivation is particularly small. The calculus will break down the formula in the following parts:

- $N0$

- Instances of $Nx \to Nsx$

- Instances of the equations $\mathcal{R}$

Assume we have a long derivation $\mathcal{D}$ of $\text{NUM} \wedge \mathcal{R} \to Nt$. Now do the following trick — substitute for each term u the value $\bar{u}$ as given by a term built up from the successor s and zero 0. Using this substitution all instances of the equations $\mathcal{R}$ will be just identities $v = v$ and are superfluous. We get a derivation $\mathcal{D}^\star$ of

$$\text{NUM} \to N\bar{t}$$

and $\mathcal{D}^\star$ is shorter than $\mathcal{D}$. In the derivation $\mathcal{D}^\star$ we must use all instances $N\bar{u} \to Ns\bar{u}$ where $\bar{u}$ is smaller than $\bar{t}$. Note that we must use all — if we for example did not use the instance $sssssssss0$ the derivation would not hold. This is bad — the derivation $\mathcal{D}^\star$ and hence also $\mathcal{D}$ must be larger than the value $\bar{t}$ of t.

One of the points of the calculus is that we could use it to give short proofs of complicated sentences. This is not possible for the calculus as it is formulated now. The problem comes from our way of building the calculus — a central point is that we start with a formula and then breaks it down into parts. The formula itself gives a way of controlling the parts which we need to consider. But this gives a calculus with too much control. In principle we can derive

$$\text{NUM} \wedge \mathcal{E} \to Neeeeee0000000$$

But the derivation is larger than the universe. In the next section we shall look at a way out.

5.6 Indirect proofs and auxiliary notions

Let us introduce some auxiliary notions:

$$N_0 x = N x$$
$$N_{n+1} x = \forall y : N_n \cdot exy : N_n$$

Here we have used $\forall y : A.fy : B$ as an abbreviation for $\forall y.(Ay \to Bfy)$ and similarly for $\forall y : N_n \cdot exy : N_n$. This does not matter. More important is the proof of the following

Lemma 5.3 *For all n NUM, $\mathcal{E} \vdash N_n 0$*

Proof. This is immediate for $n = 0$ and $n = 1$. We want to prove

$$\forall y : N_{n+1} \cdot sy : N_{n+1}$$

So assume we have y with $N_{n+1} y$. Then

$$\forall z : N_n \cdot eyz : N_n$$

and

$$\forall z : N_n \cdot eyeyz : N_n$$

specializing z to eyz. Hence $N_{n+1} sy$ and we have proved $N_{n+2} 0$. ∎

Using the lemma we get short proofs of

$$\text{NUM} \wedge \mathcal{E} \to N eeeeee0000000$$

We start with NUM, $\mathcal{E} \vdash N_6 0$. Then using NUM, $\mathcal{E} \vdash N_5 0$ we get NUM, $\mathcal{E} \vdash N_5 e00$. Going on we get NUM, $\mathcal{E} \vdash N_4 ee000$ and in the end NUM, $\mathcal{E} \vdash Neeeeee0000000$. The proof is much shorter than the value of the term. An essential ingredient in the proof is the use of the lemma.

So what is going on? Our proof system searches for direct proofs. They work as follows:

- Given a sequent Γ

- By analyzing the parts of Γ we construct a tree over it

- Hopefully the tree gives a derivation of Γ

The completeness theorem says that if Γ is valid the tree will give a derivation. But it may be quite long and the construction of the tree may be hopelessly inefficient. The tree may even be larger than the universe for some quite reasonable Γ.

It turns out that we can do better if we include some superfluous rule in our proof system

---

Cut rule:

$$\frac{\Gamma, F \quad \Gamma, \neg F}{\Gamma}$$

This rule is obviously correct — both in the synthesis and the analysis interpretation. If we just look in terms of derivability the rule is superfluous. But using it we can treat lemmas like the above. We can reformulate the rule as

$$\frac{\Gamma, \text{lemma} \quad \neg\text{lemma}, \Delta}{\Gamma, \Delta}$$

The cut rule destroys the possibility of having efficient mechanization. We start with a sequent at the root and construct step for step an analysis tree. In the cut rule there is no indication which formula F to use — we cannot in general use the conclusion Γ to find a good proposal for F. In system for mechanization of proofs this is where the interaction of the user comes in. The user helps in guessing good proposals for F.

5.7 Large numbers and fast functions

We can make notation systems where we get even larger numbers and faster functions than with the notations above. Think of multiplication $m \times n$ as built up from addition as follows

$$\underbrace{m + m + \cdots + m}_{n}$$

and similarly exponentiation $m \uparrow n$ from multiplication by

$$\underbrace{m \times m \times \cdots \times m}_{n}$$

We generalize this procedure and get $m \uparrow\uparrow n$ and $m \uparrow\uparrow\uparrow n$. Here we must be careful of how we associate the operations. Note that

$$3 \uparrow (3 \uparrow 3) = 3^{27} = 7625597484987$$
$$(3 \uparrow 3) \uparrow 3 = 27^3 = \quad 19683$$

The parentheses in our arrow notation are taken the way were it grows fastest — we evaluate from right to left. And we have

$$3 \uparrow\uparrow 3 = 7625597484987$$

These numbers grows very fast. The sequence

$$1 \uparrow 1 \ , \ 2 \uparrow\uparrow 2 \ , \ 3 \uparrow\uparrow\uparrow 3 \ , \ \cdots$$

is called the Ackermann sequence. It gives a function which grows extremely fast (faster than any function computed using only iteration).

And we have already introduced the BusyBeaver function which grows even faster.

The four main lessons

Importance of signature

The main lesson from logic is the importance of language. If we have some computational situation, then there is a formal language we can use to describe the situation — given by the signature of the language. Usually we can find the signature without too much effort and it will remain the same throughout the computation.

Syntax machines

We can think of our computations as done by syntax machines — words in and words out after having gone through a sequence of syntactical transformations. Syntax is something that can be represented by Δ_0-formulas in a data structure like the binary trees.

Using non determinacy

In our computations we use both deterministic and non deterministic transitions. One way to think of the non deterministic transitions are as delayed decisions. We can delay the decisions of which arrow to follow until the computations terminate. In this way we get a computation in the form of a tree — and can there describe both disjunctive and conjunctive non determinism.

Climbing depth first

After having defined the computation as a tree we have new algorithms opening up. Some of the most interesting comes from walking in the tree depth first.